*Voyage of
the*

JOSHUA SLOCUM

A Phoenix paperback
This edition first published in Great Britain by Phoenix,
a division of Orion Books Ltd,
Orion House, 5 Upper St Martin's Lane, London WC2H 9EA

Contains Chapters VII to XI of *Sailing Alone Around the World*

First published in Great Britain in 1900 by Sampson Low

All rights reserved. No part of this publication may be
reproduced, stored in a retrieval system, or transmitted, in
any form or by any means, electronic, mechanical,
photocopying, recording or otherwise, without the prior
permission of the copyright owner.

ISBN: 1 85799 637 2

Typeset at The Spartan Press Ltd,
Lymington, Hants
Printed in Great Britain by
Clays Ltd, St Ives plc

I

Weighing anchor at Buenos Aires – An outburst of emotion at the mouth of the Plate – Submerged by a great wave – A stormy entrance to the strait – Captain Samblich's happy gift of a bag of carpet-tacks – Off Cape Froward – Chased by Indians from Fortescue Bay – A miss-shot for 'Black Pedro' – Taking in supplies of wood and water at Three Island Cove – Animal Life.

On January 26, 1896, the *Spray*, being refitted and well provisioned in every way, sailed from Buenos Aires. There was little wind at the start; the surface of the great river was like a silver disc, and I was glad of a tow from a harbour tug to clear the port entrance. But a gale came up soon after, and caused an ugly sea, and instead of being all silver, as before, the river was now all mud. The Plate is a treacherous place for storms. One sailing there should always be on the alert for squalls. I cast anchor before dark in the best lee I could find near the land, but was tossed miserably all night, heartsore of choppy seas. On the following morning I got the sloop under way, and with reefed sails worked her down the river against a head wind. Standing in that night to the place where pilot Howard joined me for the up-river sail, I took a departure, shaping my course to clear Point Indio on the one hand, and the English Bank on the other.

I had not for many years been south of these regions. I will not say that I expected all fine sailing on the course for Cape Horn direct, but while I worked at the sails and rigging I thought only of onward and forward. It was when I anchored in the lonely places that a feeling of awe crept over me. At the last anchorage on the monotonous and muddy river, weak as it may seem, I gave way to my feelings. I resolved then that I would anchor no more north of the Strait of Magellan.

On the 28th of January the *Spray* was clear of Point Indio, English Bank, and all the other dangers of the River Plate. With a fair wind she then bore away for the Strait of Magellan, under all sail, pressing farther and farther toward the wonderland of the South, till I forgot the blessings of our milder North.

My ship passed in safety Bahia Blanca, also the Gulf of St Matias and the mighty Gulf of St George. Hoping that she might go clear of the destructive tide-races, the dread of big craft or little along this coast, I gave all the capes a berth of about fifty miles, for these dangers extend many miles from the land. But where the sloop avoided one danger she encountered another. For, one day, well off the Patagonian coast, while the sloop was reaching under short sail, a tremendous wave, the culmination, it seemed, of many waves, rolled down upon her in a storm, roaring as it came. I had only a moment to get all sail down and myself up on the peak halyards, out of danger when I saw the mighty crest towering masthead-high above me. The mountain of water submerged my vessel. She shook in every timber and reeled under the weight of the sea, but rose quickly out of it, and rode grandly over the rollers that followed. It may have been a minute that from my hold in the rigging I could see no part of the *Spray*'s hull. Perhaps it was even less time than that, but it seemed a long while, for under great excitement one lives fast, and in a few seconds one may think a great deal of one's past life. Not only did the past, with electric speed, flash before me, but I had time while in my hazardous position for resolutions for the future that would take a long time to fulfil. The first one was, I remember, that if the *Spray* came through this danger I would dedicate my best energies to building a larger ship on her lines, which I hope yet to do. Other promises, less easily kept, I should have made under protest. However, the incident, which filled me with fear, was only one more test of the *Spray*'s worthiness. It reassured me against rude Cape Horn.

From the time the great wave swept over the *Spray* until she reached Cape Virgins nothing occurred to move a pulse and set blood in motion. On the contrary, the weather became fine and the sea smooth and life tranquil. The phenomenon of mirage frequently occurred. An albatross sitting on the water one day loomed up like a large ship; two fur-seals asleep on the surface of the sea appeared like great whales, and a bank of haze I could have sworn was high land. The kaleidoscope then changed, and on the following day I sailed in a world peopled by dwarfs.

On February 11 the *Spray* rounded Cape Virgins and entered the Strait of Magellan. The scene was again real and gloomy; the wind, northeast, and blowing a gale, sent feather-white spume along the coast; such a sea ran as would swamp an ill-appointed ship. As the sloop neared the entrance to the strait I observed that two great tide-races made ahead, one very close to the point of the land and one farther offshore. Between the two, in a sort of channel, through combers, went the *Spray* with close-reefed sails. But a rolling sea followed her a long way in, and a fierce current swept around the cape against her; but this she stemmed, and was soon chirruping under the lee of Cape Virgins and running every minute into smoother water. However, long trailing kelp from sunken rocks waved forebodingly under her keel, and the wreck of a great steamship smashed on the beach abreast gave a gloomy aspect to the scene.

I was not to be let off easy. The Virgins would collect tribute even from the *Spray* passing their promontory. Fitful rain-squalls from the northwest followed the northeast gale. I reefed the sloop's sails, and sitting in the cabin to rest my eyes, I was so strongly impressed with what in all nature I might expect that as I dozed the very air I breathed seemed to warn me of danger. My senses heard '*Spray* ahoy!' shouted in warning. I sprang to the deck, wondering who could be there that knew the *Spray* so well as to call out her name passing in the dark; for it was now the blackest of nights all around, except away in the southwest where rose the old familiar white arch, the terror of Cape Horn, rapidly pushed up by a southwest gale. I had only a moment to douse sail and lash all solid when it struck like a shot from a cannon, and for the first half-hour it was something to be remembered by way of a gale. For thirty hours it kept on blowing hard. The sloop could carry no more than a three-reefed mainsail and forestaysail; with these she held on stoutly and was not blown out of the strait. In the height of the squalls in this gale she doused all sail, and this occurred often enough.

After this gale followed only a smart breeze, and the *Spray*, passing through the narrows without mishap, cast anchor at Sandy Point on February 14, 1896.

Sandy Point (Punta Arenas) is a Chilean coaling station, and boasts about two thousand inhabitants, of mixed nationality, but mostly Chileans. What with sheep-farming, gold-mining, and hunting, the settlers in this dreary land seemed not the worst off in the world. But the natives, Patagonian and Fuegian, on the other hand, were as squalid as contact with unscrupulous traders could make them. A large percentage of the business there was traffic in 'fire-water.' If there was a law against selling the poisonous stuff to the natives, it was not enforced. Fine specimens of the Patagonian race, looking smart in the morning when they came into town, had repented before night of ever having seen a white man, so beastly drunk were they, to say nothing about the peltry of which they had been robbed.

The port at that time was free, but a custom-house was in course of construction, and when it is finished, port and tariff dues are to be collected. A soldier police guarded the place, and a sort of vigilante force besides took down its guns now and then; but as a general thing, to my mind, whenever an execution was made they killed the wrong man. Just previous to my arrival the governor, himself of a jovial turn of mind, had sent a party of young bloods to foray a Fuegian settlement and wipe out what they could of it on account of the recent massacre of a schooner's crew somewhere else. Altogether the place was quite newsy and supported two papers – dailies, I think. The port captain, a Chilean naval officer, advised me to ship hands to fight Indians in the strait farther west, and spoke of my stopping until a gunboat should be going through, which would give me a tow. After canvassing the place, however, I found only one man willing to embark, and he on condition that I should sail another 'mon and a doog.' But as no one else was willing to come along, and as I drew the line at dogs, I said no more about the matter, but simply loaded my guns. At this point in my dilemma Captain Pedro Samblich, a good Austrian of large experience, coming along, gave me a bag of carpet-tacks, worth more than all the fighting men and dogs of Tierra del Fuego. I protested that I had no use for carpet-tacks on board. Samblich smiled at my want of experience, and maintained stoutly that I would have use for them. 'You must use them with discretion,' he said; 'that is to say, don't step on them yourself.' With this remote hint about the use of the tacks I got on all right, and saw the way to maintain clear decks at night without the care of watching.

Samblich was greatly interested in my voyage, and after giving me the tacks he put on board bags of biscuits and a large quantity of smoked venison. He declared that my bread, which was ordinary sea-biscuits and easily broken, was not nutritious as his, which was so hard that I could break it only with a stout blow from a maul. Then he gave me, from his own sloop, a compass which was certainly better than mine, and offered to unbend her mainsail for me if I would accept it. Last of all, this large-hearted man brought out a battle of Fuegian gold-dust from a place where it had been *cached* and begged me to help myself from it, for use farther along on the voyage. But I felt sure of success without this draft on a friend, and I was right. Samblich's tacks, as it turned out, were of more value than gold.

The port captain finding that I was resolved to go, even alone, since there was no help for it, set up no further objections, but advised me, in case the savages tried to surround me with their canoes, to shoot straight, and begin to do it in time, but to avoid killing them if possible, which I heartily agreed to do. With these simple injunctions the officer gave me my port clearance free of charge, and I sailed on the same day, February 19, 1896. It was not without thoughts of strange and stirring adventure beyond all I had yet encountered that I now sailed into the country and very core of the savage Fuegians.

A fair wind from Sandy Point brought me on the first day to St Nicholas Bay, where, so I was told, I might expect to meet savages; but seeing no signs of life, I came to anchor in eight fathoms of water, where I lay all night under a high mountain. Here I had my first experience with the terrific squalls, called williwaws, which extended from this point on through the strait to the Pacific. They were compressed gales of wind that Boreas handed down over the hills in chunks. A full-blown williwaw will throw a ship, even without sail on, over on her beam ends; but, like other gales, they cease now and then, if only for a short time.

February 20 was my birthday, and I found myself alone, with hardly so much as a bird in sight, off Cape Froward, the southernmost point of the continent of America. By daylight in the morning I was getting my ship under way for the bout ahead.

The sloop held the wind fair while she ran thirty miles farther on her course, which brought her to Fortescue Bay, and at once among the natives' signal-fires, which blazed up now on all sides. Clouds flew over the mountain from the west all day; at night my good east wind failed, and in its stead a gale from the west soon came on. I gained anchorage at twelve o'clock that night, under the lee of a little island, and then prepared myself a cup of coffee, of which I was sorely in need; for, to tell the truth, hard beating in the heavy squalls and against the current had told on my strength. Finding that the anchor held, I drank my beverage, and named the place Coffee Island. It lies to the south of Charles Island, with only a narrow channel between.

By daylight the next morning the *Spray* was again under way, beating hard; but she came to in a cove in Charles Island, two and a half miles along on her course. Here she remained undisturbed two days, with both anchors down in a bed of kelp. Indeed, she might have remained undisturbed indefinitely had not the wind moderated; for during these two days it blew so hard that no boat could venture out on the strait, and the natives being away to other hunting-grounds, the island anchorage was safe. But at the end of the fierce wind-storm fair weather came; then I got my anchors, and again sailed out upon the strait.

Canoes manned by savages from Fortescue now came in pursuit. The wind falling light they gained on me rapidly till coming within hail, when they ceased paddling, and a bow-legged savage stood up and called to me, 'Yammerschooner! yammerschooner!' which is their begging term. I said, 'No!' Now, I was not for letting on that I was alone, and so I stepped into the cabin, and, passing through the hold, came out at the fore-scuttle, changing my clothes as I went along. That made two men. Then the piece of bowsprit which I had sawed off at Buenos Aires, and which I had still on board, I arranged forward on the outlook, dressed as a seaman, attaching a line by which I could pull it into motion. That made three of us, and we didn't want to 'yammerschooner'; but for all that the savages came on faster than before. I saw that besides four at the paddles in the canoe nearest to me, there were others in the bottom, and that they were shifting hands often. At eighty yards I fired a shot across the bows of the nearest canoe, at which they all stopped, but only for a moment. Seeing that they persisted in coming nearer, I fired the second shot so close to the chap who wanted to 'yammerschooner' that he changed his mind quickly enough and bellowed in fear, 'Bueno jo via Isla,' and sitting down in his canoe, he rubbed his starboard cat-head for some time. I was thinking of the good port captain's advice when I pulled the trigger, and must have aimed pretty straight; however, a miss was as good as a mile for Mr 'Black Pedro,' as he it was, and no other, a leader in several bloody massacres. He made for the island now, and the others followed him. I knew by his Spanish lingo and by his full beard that he was the villain I had named, a renegade mongrel, and the worst murderer in Tierra del Fuego. The authorities had been in search of him for two years. The Fuegians are not bearded.

So much for the first day among the savages. I came to anchor at midnight in Three Island Cove, about twenty miles along from Fortescue Bay. I saw on the opposite side of the strait signal-fires, and heard the barking of dogs, but where I lay it was quite deserted by natives. I have always taken it as a sign that where I found birds sitting about, or seals on the rocks, I should not find savage Indians. Seals are never plentiful in these waters, but in Three Island Cove I saw one on the rocks, and other signs of the absence of savage men.

On the next day the wind was again blowing a gale, and although she was in the lee of the land, the sloop dragged her anchors, so that I had to get her under way and beat farther into the cove, where I came to in a landlocked pool. At another time or place this would have been a rash thing to do, and it was safe now only from the fact that the gale which drove me to shelter would keep the Indians from crossing the strait. Seeing this was the case, I went ashore with gun and axe on an island, where I could not in any event be surprised, and there felled trees and split about a cord of fire-wood, which loaded my small boat several times.

While I carried the wood, though I was morally sure there were no savages near, I never once went to or from the skiff without my gun. While I had that and a clear field of over eighty yards about me I felt safe.

The trees on the island, very scattering, were a sort of beech and a stunted cedar, both of which made good fuel. Even the green limbs of the beech, which seemed to possess a resinous quality, burned readily in my great drum-stove. I have described my method of wooding up in detail, that the reader who has kindly borne with me so far may see that in this, as in all other particulars of my voyage, I took great care against all kinds of surprises, whether by animals or by the elements. In the Strait of Magellan the greatest vigilance was necessary. In this instance I reasoned that I had all about me the greatest danger of the whole voyage – the treachery of cunning savages, for which I must be particularly on the alert.

The *Spray* sailed from Three Island Cove in the morning after the gale went down, but was glad to return for shelter from another sudden gale. Sailing again on the following day, she fetched Borgia Bay, a few miles on her course, where vessels had anchored from time to time and had nailed boards on the trees ashore with name and date of harbouring carved or painted. Nothing else could I see to indicate that civilized man had ever been there. I had taken a survey of the gloomy place with my spy-glass, and was getting my boat out to land and take notes, when the Chilean gunboat *Huemel* came in, and officers, coming on board, advised me to leave the place at once, a thing that required little eloquence to persuade me to do. I accepted the captain's kind offer of a tow to the next anchorage, at the place called Notch Cove, eight miles farther along, where I should be clear of the worst of the Fuegians.

We made anchorage at the cove about dark that night, while the wind came down in fierce williwaws from the mountains. An instance of Magellan weather was afforded when the *Huemel*, a well-appointed gunboat of great power, after attempting on the following day to proceed on her voyage, was obliged by sheer force of the wind to return and take up anchorage again and remain till the gale abated; and lucky she was to get back!

Meeting this vessel was a little godsend. She was commanded and officered by high-class sailors and educated gentlemen. An entertainment that was gotten up on her, impromptu, at the Notch would be hard to beat anywhere. One of her midshipmen sang popular songs in French, German, and Spanish, and one (so he said) in Russian. If the audience did not know the lingo of one song from another, it was no drawback to the merriment.

I was left alone the next day, for then the *Huemel* put out on her voyage, the gale having abated. I spent a day taking in wood and water; by the end of that time the weather was fine. Then I sailed from the desolate place.

There is little more to be said concerning the *Spray*'s first passage through the strait that would differ from what I have already recorded. She anchored and weighed many times, and beat many days against the current, with now and then a 'slant' for a few miles, till finally she gained anchorage and shelter for the night at Port Tamar, with Cape Pillar in sight to the west. Here I felt the throb of the great ocean that lay before me. I knew now that I had put a world behind me, and that I was opening out another world ahead. I had passed the haunts of savages. Great piles of granite mountains of bleak and lifeless aspect were now astern; on some of them not even a speck of moss had ever grown. There was an unfinished newness all about the land. On the hill back of Port Tamar a small beacon had been thrown up showing that some man had been there. But how could one tell but that he had died of loneliness and grief? In a bleak land is not the place to enjoy solitude.

Throughout the whole of the strait west of Cape Froward I saw no animals except dogs owned by savages. These I saw often enough, and heard them yelping night and day. Birds were not plentiful. The scream of a wild fowl, which I took for a loon, sometimes startled me with its piercing cry. The steamboat duck, so called because it propels itself over the sea with its wings, and resembles a miniature side-wheel steamer in its motion, was sometimes seen scurrying on out of danger. It never flies, but, hitting the water instead of the air with its wings, it moves faster than a rowboat or a canoe. The few fur-seals I saw were very shy; and of fishes I saw next to none at all. I did not catch one; indeed, I seldom or never put a hook over during the whole voyage. Here in the strait I found great abundance of mussels of an excellent quality. I fared sumptuously on them. There was a sort of swan, smaller than a Muscovy duck, which might have been brought down with the gun, but in the loneliness of life about the dreary country I found myself in no mood to make one life less, except in self-defence.

II

From Cape Pillar into the Pacific – Driven by a tempest toward Cape Horn – Captain Slocum's greatest sea adventure – Reaching the strait again by way of Cockburn Channel – Some savages find the carpet-tacks – Danger from firebrands – A series of fierce williwaws – Again sailing westward.

It was the 3rd of March when the *Spray* sailed from Port Tamar direct for Cape Pillar, with the wind from the northeast, which I fervently hoped might hold till she cleared the land; but there was no such good luck in store. It soon began to rain and thicken in the northwest, boding no good. The *Spray* neared Cape Pillar rapidly, and, nothing loath, plunged into the Pacific Ocean at once, taking her first bath of it in the gathering storm. There was no turning back even had I wished to do so, for the land was now shut out by the darkness of night. The wind freshened, and I took in a third reef. The sea was confused and treacherous. In such a time as this the old fisherman prayed, 'Remember, Lord, my ship is so small and thy sea is so wide!' I saw now only the gleaming crests of waves.

They showed white teeth while the sloop balanced over them. 'Everything for an offing,' I cried, and to this end I carried on all the sail she would bear. She ran all night with a free sheet, but on the morning of March 4 the wind shifted to southwest, then back suddenly to northwest, and blew with terrific force. The *Spray*, stripped of her sails, then bore off under bare poles. No ship in the world could have stood up against so violent a gale. Knowing that this storm might continue for many days, and that it would be impossible to work back to the westward along the coast outside of Tierra del Fuego, there seemed nothing to do but to keep on and go east about, after all. Anyhow, for my present safety the only course lay in keeping her before the wind. And so she drove southeast, as though about to round the Horn, while the waves rose and fell and bellowed their never-ending story of the sea; but the Hand that held these held also the *Spray*. She was running now with a reefed forestaysail, the sheets flat amidship. I paid out two long ropes to steady her course and to break combing seas astern, and I lashed the helm amidship. In this trim she ran before it, shipping never a sea. Even while the storm raged at its worst, my ship was wholesome and noble. My mind as to her seaworthiness was put to ease for aye.

When all had been done that I could do for the safety of the vessel, I got to the fore-scuttle, between seas, and prepared a pot of coffee over a wood fire, and made a good Irish stew. Then, as before and afterward on the *Spray*, I insisted on warm meals. In the tide-race off Cape Pillar, however, where the sea was marvellously high, uneven, and crooked, my appetite was slim, and for a time I postponed cooking. (Confidentially, I was seasick!)

The first day of the storm gave the *Spray* her actual test in the worst sea that Cape Horn or its wild regions could afford, and in no part of the world could a rougher sea be found than at this particular point, namely, off Cape Pillar, the grim sentinel of the Horn.

Farther offshore, while the sea was majestic, there was less apprehension of danger. There the *Spray* rode, now like a bird on the crest of a wave, and now like a waif deep down in the hollow between seas; and so she drove on. Whole days passed, counted as other days, but with always a thrill – yes, of delight.

On the fourth day of the gale, rapidly nearing the pitch of Cape Horn, I inspected my chart and pricked off the course and distance to Port Stanley, in the Falkland Islands, where I might find my way and refit, when I saw through a rift in the clouds a high mountain, about seven leagues away on the port beam. The fierce edge of the gale by this time had blown off, and I had already bent a square-sail on the boom in place of the mainsail, which was torn to rags. I hauled in the trailing ropes, hoisted this awkward sail reefed, the forestaysail being already set, and under this sail brought her at once on the wind heading for the land, which appeared as an island in the sea. So it turned out to be, though not the one I had supposed.

I was exultant over the prospect of once more entering the Strait of Magellan and beating through again into the Pacific, for it was more than rough on the outside coast of Tierra del Fuego. It was indeed a mountainous sea. When the sloop was in the fiercest squalls, with only the reefed forestaysail set, even that small sail shook her from keelson to truck when it shivered by the leech. Had I harboured the shadow of a doubt for her safety, it would have been that she might spring a leak in the garboard at the heel of the mast; but she never called me once to the pump. Under pressure of the smallest sail I could set she made for the land like a race-horse, and steering her over the crests of the waves so that she might not trip was nice work. I stood at the helm now and made the most of it.

Night closed in before the sloop reached the land, leaving her feeling the way in pitchy darkness. I saw breakers ahead before long. At this I wore ship and stood offshore, but was immediately startled by the tremendous roaring of breakers again ahead and on the lee bow. This puzzled me, for there should have been no broken water where I supposed myself to be. I kept off a good bit, then wore round, but finding broken water also there, threw her head again offshore. In this way, among dangers, I spent the rest of the night. Hail and sleet in the fierce squalls cut my flesh till the blood trickled over my face; but what of that? It was daylight, and the sloop was in the midst of the Milky Way of the sea, which is northwest of Cape Horn, and it was the white breakers of a huge sea over sunken rocks which had threatened to engulf her through the night. It was Fury Island I had sighted and steered for, and what a panorama was before me now and all around! It was not the time to complain of a broken skin. What could I do but fill away among the breakers and find a channel between them, now that it was day? Since she had escaped the rocks through the night, surely she would find her way by daylight. This was the greatest sea adventure of my life. God knows how my vessel escaped.

The sloop at last reached inside of small islands that sheltered her in smooth water. Then I climbed the mast to survey the wild scene astern. The great naturalist Darwin looked over this seascape from the deck of the *Beagle*, and wrote in his journal, 'Any landsman seeing the Milky Way would have nightmare for a week.' He might have added 'or seaman' as well.

The *Spray*'s good luck followed fast. I discovered, as she sailed along through a labyrinth of islands, that she was in the Cockburn Channel, which leads into the Strait of Magellan at a point opposite Cape Froward, and that she was already passing Thieves' Bay, suggestively named. And at night, March 8, behold, she was at anchor in a snug cove at the Turn! Every heartbeat on the *Spray* now counted thanks.

Here I pondered on the events of the last few days, and, strangely enough, instead of feeling rested from sitting or lying down, I now began to feel jaded and worn; but a hot meal of venison stew soon put me right, so that I could sleep. As drowsiness came on I sprinkled the deck with tacks, and then I turned in, bearing in mind the advice of my old friend Samblich that I was not to step on them myself. I saw to it that not a few of them stood 'business end' up; for when the *Spray* passed Thieves' Bay two canoes had put out and followed in her wake, and there was no disguising the fact any longer that I was alone.

Now, it is well known that one cannot step on a tack without saying something about it. A pretty good Christian will whistle when he steps on the 'commercial end' of a carpet-tack; a savage will howl and claw the air, and that was just what happened that night about twelve o'clock, while I was asleep in the cabin, where the savages thought they 'had me,' sloop and all, but changed their minds when they stepped on deck, for then they thought that I or somebody else had them. I had no need of a dog; they howled like a pack of hounds. I had hardly use for a gun. They jumped pellmell, some into their canoes and some into the sea, to cool off, I suppose, and there was a deal of free language over it as they went. I fired several guns when I came on deck, to let the rascals know that I was home, and then I turned in again, feeling sure I should not be disturbed any more by people who left in so great a hurry.

The Fuegians, being cruel, are naturally cowards; they regard a rifle with superstitious fear. The only real danger one could see that might come from their quarter would be from allowing them to surround one within bow-shot, or to anchor within range where they might lie in ambush. As for their coming on deck at night, even had I not put tacks about, I could have cleared them off by shots from the cabin and hold. I always kept a quantity of ammunition within reach in the hold and in the cabin and in the forepeak, so that retreating to any of these places I could 'hold the fort' simply by shooting up through the deck.

Perhaps the greatest danger to be apprehended was from the use of fire. Every canoe carries fire; nothing is thought of that, for it is their custom to communicate by smoke-signals. The harmless brand that lies smouldering in the bottom of one of their canoes might be ablaze in one's cabin if he were not on the alert. The port captain of Sandy Point warned me particularly of this danger. Only a short time before they had fired a Chilean gunboat by throwing brands in through the stern windows of the cabin. The *Spray* had no openings in the cabin or deck, except two scuttles, and these were guarded by fastenings which could not be undone without waking me if I were asleep.

On the morning of the 9th, after a refreshing rest and a warm breakfast, and after I had swept the deck of tacks, I got out what spare canvas there was on board, and began to sew the pieces together in the shape of a peak for my square-mainsail, the tarpaulin. The day to all appearances promised fine weather and light winds, but appearances in Tierra del Fuego do not always count. While I was wondering why no trees grew on the slope abreast of the anchorage, half minded to lay by the sail-making and land with my gun for some game and to inspect a white boulder on the beach, near the brook, a williwaw came down with such terrific force as to carry the *Spray*, with two anchors down, like a feather out of the cove and away into deep water. No wonder trees did not grow on the side of that hill! Great Boreas! a tree would need to be all roots to hold on against such a furious wind.

From the cove to the nearest land to leeward was a long drift, however, and I had ample time to weigh both anchors before the sloop came near any danger, and so no harm came of it. I saw no more savages that day or the next; they probably had some sign by which they knew of the coming williwaws; at least, they were wise in not being afloat even on the second day, for I had no sooner gotten to work at sail-making again, after the anchor was down, than the wind, as on the day before, picked the sloop up and flung her seaward with a vengeance, anchor and all, as before. This fierce wind, usual to the Magellan country, continued on through the day, and swept the sloop by several miles of steep bluffs and precipices overhanging a bold shore of wild and uninviting appearance. I was not sorry to get away from it, though in doing so it was no Elysian shore to which I shaped my course. I kept on sailing in hope, since I had no choice but to go on, heading across for St Nicholas Bay, where I had cast anchor February 19. It was now the 10th of March! Upon reaching the bay the second time I had circumnavigated the wildest part of desolate Tierra del Fuego. But the *Spray* had not yet arrived at St Nicholas, and by the merest accident her bones were saved from resting there when she did arrive. The parting of a staysailsheet in a williwaw, when the sea was turbulent and she was plunging into the storm, brought me forward to see instantly a dark cliff ahead and breakers so close under the bows that I felt surely lost, and in my thoughts cried, 'Is the hand of fate against me, after all, leading me in the end to this dark spot?' I sprang aft again, unheeding the flapping sail, and threw the wheel over, expecting, as the sloop came down into the hollow of a wave, to feel her timbers smash under me on the rocks. But at the touch of her helm she swung clear of the danger, and in the next moment she was in the lee of the land.

It was the small island in the middle of the bay for which the sloop had been steering, and which she made with such unerring aim as nearly to run it down. Farther along in the bay was the anchorage, which I managed to reach, but before I could get the anchor down another squall caught the sloop and whirled her round like a top and carried her away, altogether to leeward of the bay. Still farther to leeward was a great headland, and I bore off for that. This was retracing my course toward Sandy Point, for the gale was from the southwest.

I had the sloop soon under good control, however, and in a short time rounded to under the lee of a mountain, where the sea was as smooth as a mill-pond, and the sails flapped and hung limp while she carried her way close in. Here I thought I would anchor and rest till morning, the depth being eight fathoms very close to the shore. But it was interesting to see, as I let go the anchor, that it did not reach the bottom before another williwaw struck down from this mountain and carried the sloop off faster than I could pay out cable. Therefore, instead of resting, I had to 'man the windlass' and heave up the anchor with fifty fathoms of cable hanging up and down in deep water. This was in that part of the strait called Famine Reach. Dismal Famine Reach! On the sloop's crab-windlass I worked the rest of the night, thinking how much easier it was for me when I could say, 'Do that thing or the other,' than now doing all myself. But I hove away and sang the old chants that I sang when I was a sailor. Within the last few days I had passed through much and was now thankful that my state was no worse.

It was daybreak when the anchor was at the hawse. By this time the wind had gone down, and cat's-paws took the place of williwaws, while the sloop drifted slowly toward Sandy Point. She came within sight of ships at anchor in the roads, and I was more than half minded to put in for new sails, but the wind coming out from the northeast, which was fair for the other direction, I turned the prow of the *Spray* westward once more for the Pacific, to traverse a second time the second half of my first course through the strait.

III

Repairing the *Spray*'s sails – Savages and an obstreperous anchor – A spider-fight – An encounter with Black Pedro – A visit to the steamship *Colombia* – On the defensive against a fleet of canoes – A record of voyages through the strait – A chance cargo of tallow.

I was determined to rely on my own small resources to repair the damages of the great gale which drove me southward toward the Horn, after I had passed from the Strait of Magellan out into the Pacific. So when I had got back into the strait, by way of Cockburn Channel, I did not proceed eastward for help at the Sandy Point settlement, but turning again into the northwestward reach of the strait, set to work with my palm and needle at every opportunity, when at anchor and when sailing. It was slow work; but little by little the squaresail on the boom expanded to the dimensions of a serviceable mainsail with a peak to it and a leech besides. If it was not the best-setting sail afloat, it was at least very strongly made and would stand a hard blow. A ship, meeting the *Spray* long afterward, reported her as wearing a mainsail of some improved design and patent reefer, but that was not the case.

The *Spray* for a few days after the storm enjoyed fine weather, and made fair time through the strait for the distance of twenty miles, which, in these days of many adversities, I called a long run. The weather, I say, was fine for a few days; but it brought little rest. Care for the safety of my vessel, and even for my own life, was in no wise lessened by the absence of heavy weather. Indeed, the peril was even greater, inasmuch as the savages on comparatively fine days ventured forth on their marauding excursions, and in boisterous weather disappeared from sight, their wretched canoes being frail and undeserving the name of craft at all. This being so, I now enjoyed gales of wind as never before, and the *Spray* was never long without them during her struggles about Cape Horn. I became in a measure inured to the life, and began to think that one more trip through the strait, if perchance the sloop should be blown off again, would make me the aggressor, and put the Fuegians entirely on the defensive. This feeling was forcibly borne in on me at Snug Bay, where I anchored at grey morning after passing Cape Froward, to find, when broad day appeared, that two canoes which I had eluded by sailing all night were now entering the same bay stealthily under the shadow of the high headland. They were well manned, and the savages were well armed with spears and bows. At a shot from my rifle across the bows, both turned aside into a small creek out of range. In danger now of being flanked by the savages in the bush close aboard, I was obliged to hoist the sails, which I had barely lowered, and make across to the opposite side of the strait, a distance of six miles. But now I was put to my wit's end as to how I should weigh anchor, for through an accident to the windlass right here I could not budge it. However, I set all sail and filled away, first hauling short by hand. The sloop carried her anchor away, as though it was meant to be always towed in this way underfoot, and with it she towed a ton or more of kelp from a reef in the bay, the wind blowing a wholesale breeze.

Meanwhile I worked till blood started from my fingers, and with one eye over my shoulder for savages, I watched at the same time, and sent a bullet whistling whenever I saw a limb or a twig move; for I kept a gun always at hand, and an Indian appearing then within range would have been taken as a declaration of war. As it was, however, my own blood was all that was spilt – and from the trifling accident of sometimes breaking the flesh against a cleat or a pin which came in the way when I was in haste. Sea-cuts in my hands from pulling on hard, wet ropes were sometimes painful and often bled freely; but these healed when I finally got away from the strait into fine weather.

After clearing Snug Bay I hauled the sloop to the wind, repaired the windlass, and hove the anchor to the hawse, catted it, and then stretched across to a port of refuge under a high mountain about six miles away, and came to in nine fathoms close under the face of a perpendicular cliff. Here my own voice answered back, and I named the place 'Echo Mountain.' Seeing dead trees farther along where the shore was broken, I made a landing for fuel, taking, besides my axe, a rifle, which on these days I never left far from hand; but I saw no living thing here, except a small spider, which had nested in a dry log that I boated to the sloop. The conduct of this insect interested me now more than anything else around the wild place. In my cabin it met, oddly enough, a spider of its own size and species that had come all the way from Boston – a very civil little chap, too, but mighty spry. Well, the Fuegian threw up its antennae for a fight; but my little Bostonian downed it at once, then broke its legs, and pulled them off, one by one, so dexterously that in less than three minutes from the time the battle began the Fuegian spider didn't know itself from a fly.

I made haste the following morning to be under way after a night of wakefulness on the weird shore. Before weighing anchor, however, I prepared a cup of warm coffee over a smart wood fire in my great Montevideo stove. In the same fire was cremated the Fuegian spider, slain the day before by the little warrior from Boston, which a Scots lady at Cape Town long after named 'Bruce' upon hearing of its prowess at Echo Mountain. The *Spray* now reached away for Coffee Island, which I sighted on my birthday, February 20, 1896.

There she encountered another gale, that brought her in

the lee of great Charles Island for shelter. On a bluff point on Charles were signal-fires, and a tribe of savages, mustered here since my first trip through the strait, manned their canoes to put off for the sloop. It was not prudent to come to, the anchorage being within bow-shot of the shore, which was thickly wooded; but I made signs that one canoe might come alongside, while the sloop ranged about under sail in the lee of the land. The others I motioned to keep off, and incidentally laid a smart Martini-Henry rifle in sight, close at hand, on the top of the cabin. In the canoe that came alongside, crying their never-ending begging word 'yammerschooner,' were two squaws and one Indian, the hardest specimens of humanity I had ever seen in any of my travels. 'Yammerschooner' was their plaint when they pushed off from the shore, and 'yammershooner' it was when they got alongside. The squaws beckoned for food, while the Indian, a black-visaged savage, stood sulkily as if he took no interest at all in the matter, but on my turning my back for some biscuits and jerked beef for the squaws, the 'buck' sprang on deck and confronted me, saying in Spanish jargon that we had met before. I thought I recognized the tone of his 'yammerschooner,' and his full beard identified him as the Black Pedro whom, it was true, I had met before. 'Where are the rest of the crew?' he asked, as he looked uneasily around, expecting hands, maybe, to come out of the fore-scuttle and deal him his just deserts for many murders. 'About three weeks ago,' said he, 'when you passed up here, I saw three men on board. Where are the other two?' I answered him briefly that the same crew was still on board. 'But,' said he, 'I see you are doing all the work,' and with a leer he added, as he glanced at the mainsail, 'hombre valiente.' I explained that I did all the work in the day, while the rest of the crew slept, so that they would be fresh to watch for Indians at night. I was interested in the subtle cunning of this savage, knowing him, as I did, better perhaps than he was aware. Even had I not been advised before I sailed from Sandy Point, I should have measured him for an arch-villain now. Moreover, one of the squaws, with that spark of kindliness which is somehow found in the breast of even the lowest savage, warned me by a sign to be on my guard, or Black Pedro would do me harm. There was no need of the warning, however, for I was on my guard from the first, and at that moment held a smart revolver in my hand ready for instant service.

'When you sailed through here before,' he said, 'you fired a shot at me,' adding with some warmth that it was 'muy malo.' I affected not to understand, and said, 'You have lived at Sandy Point, have you not?' He answered frankly, 'Yes,' and appeared delighted to meet one who had come from the dear old place. 'At the mission?' I queried. 'Why, yes,' he replied, stepping forward as if to embrace an old friend. I motioned him back, for I did not share his flattering humour. 'And you know Captain Pedro Samblich?' continued I. 'Yes,' said the villain, who had killed a kinsman of Samblich – 'yes, indeed; he is a great friend of mine.' 'I know it,' said I. Samblich had told me to shoot him on sight. Pointing to my rifle on the cabin, he wanted to know how many times it fired. 'Cuantos?' said he. When I explained to him that that gun kept right on shooting, his jaw fell, and he spoke of getting away. I did not hinder him from going. I gave the squaws biscuits and beef, and one of them gave me several lumps of tallow in exchange, and I think it worth mentioning that she did not offer me the smallest pieces, but with some extra trouble handed me the largest of all the pieces in the canoe. No Christian could have done more. Before pushing off from the sloop the cunning savage asked for matches, and made as if to reach with the end of his spear the box I was about to give him; but I held it toward him on the muzzle of my rifle, the one that 'kept on shooting.' The chap picked the box off the gun gingerly enough, to be sure, but he jumped when I said, 'Quedao' [Look out], at which the squaws laughed and seemed not at all displeased. Perhaps the wretch had clubbed them that morning for not gathering mussels enough for his breakfast. There was a good understanding among us all.

From Charles Island the *Spray* crossed over to Fortescue Bay, where she anchored and spent a comfortable night under the lee of high land, while the wind howled outside. The bay was deserted now. They were Fortescue Indians whom I had seen at the island, and I felt quite sure they could not follow the *Spray* in the present hard blow. Not to neglect a precaution, however, I sprinkled tacks on deck before I turned in.

On the following day the loneliness of the place was broken by the appearance of a great steamship, making for the anchorage with a lofty bearing. She was no Diego craft. I knew the sheer, the model, and the poise. I threw out my flag, and directly saw the Stars and Stripes flung to the breeze from the great ship.

The wind had then abated, and toward night the savages made their appearance from the island, going direct to the steamer to 'yammerschooner.' Then they came to the *Spray* to beg more, or to steal all, declaring that they got nothing from the steamer. Black Pedro here came alongside again. My own brother could not have been more delighted to see me, and he begged me to lend him my rifle to shoot a guanaco for me in the morning. I assured the fellow that if I remained there another day I would lend him the gun, but I had no mind to remain. I gave him a cooper's draw-knife and some other small implements which would be of service in canoe-making, and bade him be off.

Under the cover of darkness that night I went to the steamer, which I found to be the *Colombia*, Captain Henderson, from New York, bound for San Francisco. I carried all my guns along with me, in case it should be necessary to fight my way back. In the chief mate of the *Colombia*, Mr Hannibal, I found an old friend, and he referred affectionately to days in Manila when we were there together, he in the *Southern Cross* and I in the *Northern Light*, both ships as beautiful as their names.

The *Colombia* had an abundance of fresh stores on board. The captain gave his steward some order, and I remember that the guileless young man asked me if I could manage, besides other things, a few cans of milk and a cheese. When I offered my Montevideo gold for the supplies, the captain roared like a lion and told me to put my money up. It was a glorious outfit of provisions of all kinds that I got.

Returning to the *Spray*, where I found all secure, I prepared for an early start in the morning. It was agreed that the steamer should blow her whistle for me if first on the move. I watched the steamer, off and on, through the night for the pleasure alone of seeing her electric lights, a pleasing sight in contrast to the ordinary Fuegian canoe with a brand of fire in it. The sloop was the first under way, but the *Colombia*, soon following, passed, and saluted as she went by. Had the captain given me his steamer, his company would have been no worse off than they were two or three months later. I read afterward, in a late California paper, 'The *Colombia* will be a total loss.' On her second trip to Panama she was wrecked on the rocks of the California coast.

The *Spray* was then beating against wind and current, as usual in the strait. At this point the tides from the Atlantic and the Pacific meet, and in the strait, as on the outside coast, their meeting makes a commotion of whirlpools and combers that in a gale of wind is dangerous to canoes and other frail craft.

A few miles farther along was a large steamer ashore, bottom up. Passing this place, the sloop ran into a streak of light wind, and then — a most remarkable condition for strait weather — it fell entirely calm. Signal-fires sprang up at once on all sides, and then more than twenty canoes hove in sight, all heading for the *Spray*. As they came within hail, their savage crews cried, 'Amigo yammerschooner,' 'Anclas aqui,' 'Bueno puerto aqui,' and like scraps of Spanish mixed with their own jargon. I had no thought of anchoring in their 'good port.' I hoisted the sloop's flag and fired a gun, all of which they might construe as a friendly salute or an invitation to come on. They drew up in a semicircle, but kept outside of eighty yards, which in self-defence would have been the death-line.

In their mosquito fleet was a ship's boat stolen probably from a murdered crew. Six savages paddled this rather awkwardly with the blades of oars which had been broken off. Two of the savages standing erect wore sea-boots, and this sustained the suspicion that they had fallen upon some luckless ship's crew, and also added a hint that they had already visited the *Spray's* deck, and would now, if they could, try her again. Their sea-boots, I have no doubt, would have protected their feet and rendered carpet-tacks harmless. Paddling clumsily, they passed down the strait at a distance of a hundred yards from the sloop, in an offhand manner and as if bound to Fortescue Bay. This I judged to be a piece of strategy, and so kept a sharp lookout over a small island which soon came in range between them and the sloop, completely hiding them from view, and toward which the *Spray* was now drifting helplessly with the tide, and with every prospect of going on the rocks, for there was no anchorage, at least, none that my cables would reach. And, sure enough, I soon saw a movement in the grass just on top of the island, which is called Bonet Island and is one hundred and thirty-six feet high. I fired several shots over the place, but saw no other sign of the savages. It was they that had moved the grass, for as the sloop swept past the island, the rebound of the tide carrying her clear, there on the other side was the boat, surely enough exposing their cunning and treachery. A stiff breeze, coming up suddenly, now scattered the canoes while it extricated the sloop from a dangerous position, albeit the wind, though friendly, was still ahead.

The *Spray*, flogging against current and wind, made Borgia Bay on the following afternoon, and cast anchor there for the second time. I would now, if I could, describe the moonlit scene on the strait at midnight after I had cleared the savages and Bonet Island. A heavy cloud-bank that had swept across the sky then cleared away, and the night became suddenly as light as day, or nearly so. A high mountain was mirrored in the channel ahead, and the *Spray* sailing along with her shadow was as two sloops on the sea.

The sloop being moored, I threw out my skiff, and with

axe and gun landed at the head of the cove, and filled a barrel of water from a stream. Then, as before, there was no sign of Indians at the place. Finding it quite deserted, I rambled about near the beach for an hour or more. The fine weather seemed, somehow, to add loneliness to the place, and when I came upon a spot where a grave was marked I went no farther. Returning to the head of the cove, I came to a sort of Calvary, it appeared to me, where navigators, carrying their cross, had each set one up as a beacon to others coming after. They had anchored here and gone on, all except the one under the little mound. One of the simple marks, curiously enough, had been left there by the steamship *Colimbia*, sister ship to the *Colombia*, my neighbour of that morning.

I read the names of many other vessels; some of them I copied in my journal, others were illegible. Many of the crosses had decayed and fallen, and many a hand that put them there I had known, many a hand now still. The air of depression was about the place, and I hurried back to the sloop to forget myself again in the voyage.

Early the next morning I stood out from Borgia Bay, and off Cape Quod, where the wind fell light, I moored the sloop by kelp in twenty fathoms of water, and held her there a few hours against a three-knot current. That night I anchored in Langara Cove, a few miles farther along, where on the following day I discovered wreckage and goods washed up from the sea. I worked all day now, salving and boating off a cargo to the sloop. The bulk of the goods was tallow in casks and in lumps from which the casks had broken away; and embedded in the seaweed was a barrel of wine, which I also towed alongside. I hoisted them all in with the throat-halyards, which I took to the windlass. The weight of some of the casks was a little over eight hundred pounds.

There were no Indians about Langara; evidently there had not been any since the great gale which had washed the wreckage on shore. Probably it was the same gale that drove the *Spray* off Cape Horn from March 3 to 8. Hundreds of tons of kelp had been torn from beds in deep water and rolled up into ridges on the beach. A specimen stalk which I found entire, roots, leaves, and all, measured one hundred and thirty-one feet in length. At this place I filled a barrel of water at night, and on the following day sailed with a fair wind at last.

I had not sailed far, however, when I came abreast of more tallow in a small cove, where I anchored, and boated off as before. It rained and snowed hard all that day, and it was no light work carrying tallow in my arms over the boulders on the beach. But I worked on till the *Spray* was loaded with a full cargo. I was happy then in the prospect of doing a good business farther along on the voyage, for the habits of an old trader would come to the surface. I sailed from the cove about noon, greased from top to toe, while my vessel was tallowed from keelson to truck. My cabin, as well as the hold and deck, was stowed full of tallow, and all were thoroughly smeared.

IV

Running to Port Angosto in a snow-storm – A defective sheet-rope places the *Spray* in peril – The *Spray* as a target for a Fuegian arrow – The island of Alan Erric – Again in the open Pacific – The run to the island of Juan Fernandez – An absentee king – At Robinson Crusoe's anchorage.

Another gale had then sprang up, but the wind was still fair, and I had only twenty-six miles to run for Port Angosto, a dreary enough place, where, however, I would find a safe harbour in which to refit and stow cargo. I carried on sail to make the harbour before dark, and she fairly flew along, all covered with snow, which fell thick and fast, till she looked like a white winter bird. Between the storm-bursts I saw the headland of my port, and was steering for it when a flaw of wind caught the mainsail by the lee, jibed it over, and dear! dear! how nearly was this the cause of disaster; for the sheet parted and the boom unshipped, and it was then close upon night. I worked till the perspiration poured from my body, to get things adjusted and in working order before dark, and, above all, to get it done before the sloop drove to leeward of the port of refuge. Even then I did not get the boom shipped in its saddle. I was at the entrance of the harbour before I could get this done, and it was time to haul her to or lose the port; but in that condition, like a bird with a broken wing, she made the haven. The accident which so jeopardized my vessel and cargo came of a defective sheet-rope, one made from sisal, a treacherous fibre which has caused a deal of strong language among sailors.

I did not run the *Spray* into the inner harbour of Port Angosto, but came to inside a bed of kelp under a steep bluff on the port hand going in. It was an exceedingly snug nook, and to make doubly sure of holding on here against all williwaws I moored her with two anchors and secured her, besides, by cables to trees. However, no wind ever reached there except back flaws from the mountains on the opposite side of the harbour. There, as elsewhere in that region, the country was made up of mountains. This was the place where I was to refit and whence I was to sail direct, once more, for Cape Pillar and the Pacific.

I remained at Port Angosto some days, busily employed about the sloop. I stowed the tallow from the deck to the hold, arranged my cabin in better order, and took in a good supply of wood and water. I also mended the sloop's sails and rigging, and fitted a jigger, which changed the rig to a yawl, though I called the boat a sloop just the same, the jigger being merely a temporary affair.

I never forgot, even at the busiest time of my work there, to have my rifle by me ready for instant use; for I was of necessity within range of savages, and I had seen Fuegian canoes at this place when I anchored in the port, farther down the reach, on the first trip through the strait. I think it was on the second day, while I was busily employed about decks, that I heard the swish of something through the air close by my ear, and heard a 'zip'-like sound in the water, but saw nothing. Presently, however, I suspected that it was an arrow of some sort, for just then one passing not far from me struck the mainmast, where it stuck fast, vibrating from the shock – a Fuegian autograph. A savage was somewhere near, there could be no doubt about that. I did not know but he might be shooting at me, with a view to getting my sloop and her cargo; and so I threw up my old Martini-Henry, the rifle that kept on shooting, and the first shot uncovered three Fuegians, who scampered from a clump of bushes where they had been concealed, and made over the hills. I fired away a good many cartridges, aiming under their feet to encourage their climbing. My dear old gun woke up the hills, and at every report all three of the savages jumped as if shot; but they kept on, and put Fuego real estate between themselves and the *Spray* as fast as their legs could carry them. I took care then, more than ever before, that all my firearms should be in order and that a supply of ammunition should always be ready at hand. But the savages did not return, and although I put tacks on deck every night, I never discovered that any more visitors came, and I had only to sweep the deck of tacks carefully every morning after.

As the days went by, the season became more favourable for a chance to clear the strait with a fair wind, and so I made up my mind after six attempts, being driven back each time, to be in no further haste to sail. The bad weather on my last return to Port Angosto for shelter brought the Chilean gunboat *Condor* and the Argentine cruiser *Azopardo* into port. As soon as the latter came to anchor, Captain Mascarella, the commander, sent a boat to the *Spray* with a message that he would take me in tow for Sandy Point if I would give up the voyage and return – the thing farthest from my mind. The officers of the *Azopardo* told me that, coming up the strait after the *Spray* on her first passage through, they saw Black Pedro and learned that he had visited me. The *Azopardo*, being a foreign man-of-war, had no right to arrest the Fuegian outlaw, but her captain blamed me for not shooting the rascal when he came to my sloop.

I procured some cordage and other small supplies from these vessels, and the officers of each of them mustered a supply of warm flannels, of which I was most in need. With these additions to my outfit, and with the vessel in good trim, though somewhat deeply laden, I was well prepared for another bout with the Southern, misnamed Pacific, Ocean.

In the first week in April southeast winds, such as appear about Cape Horn in the fall and winter seasons, bringing better weather than that experienced in the summer began to disturb the upper clouds; a little more patience, and the time would come for sailing with a fair wind.

At Port Angosto I met Professor Dusen of the Swedish scientific expedition to South America and the Pacific Islands. The professor was camped by the side of a brook at the head of the harbour, where there were many varieties of moss, in which he was interested, and where the water was, as his Argentine cook said, 'muy rico.' The professor had three well-armed Argentines along in his camp to fight savages. They seemed disgusted when I filled water at a small stream near the vessel, slighting their advice to go farther up to the greater brook, where it was 'muy rico.' But they were all fine fellows, though it was a wonder that they did not all die of rheumatic pains from living on wet ground.

Of all the little haps and mishaps to the *Spray* at Port Angosto, of the many attempts to put to sea, and of each return for shelter, it is not my purpose to speak. Of hindrances there were many to keep her back, but on the thirteenth day of April, and for the seventh and last time, she weighed anchor from that port. Difficulties, however, multiplied all about in so strange a manner that had I been given to superstitious fears I should not have persisted in sailing on a thirteenth day, notwithstanding that a fair wind blew in the offing. Many of the incidents were ludicrous. When I found myself, for instance, disentangling the sloop's mast from the branches of a tree after she had drifted three times around a small island, against my will, it seemed more than one's nerves could bear, and I had to speak about it, so I thought, or die of lockjaw, and I apostrophized the *Spray* as an impatient farmer might his horse or his ox. 'Didn't you know,' cried I – 'didn't you know that you couldn't climb a tree?' But the poor old *Spray* had essayed, and successfully too, nearly everything else in the Strait of Magellan, and my heart softened toward her when I thought of what she had gone through. Moreover, she had discovered an island. On the charts this one that she had sailed around was traced as a point of land. I named it Alan Erric Island, after a worthy literary friend whom I had met in strange by-places, and I put up a sign, 'Keep off the grass,' which, as discoverer, was within my rights.

Now at last the *Spray* carried me free of Tierra del Fuego. If by a close shave only, still she carried me clear, though her boom actually hit the beacon rocks to leeward as she lugged on sail to clear the point. The thing was done on the 13th of April, 1896. But a close shave and a narrow escape were nothing new to the *Spray*.

The waves doffed their white caps beautifully to her in the strait that day before the southeast wind, the first true winter breeze of the season from that quarter, and here she was out on the first of it, with every prospect of clearing Cape Pillar before it should shift. So it turned out; the wind blew hard, as it always blows about Cape Horn, but she had cleared the great tide-race off Cape Pillar and the Evangelistas, the outermost rocks of all, before the change came. I remained at the helm, humouring my vessel in the cross seas, for it was rough, and I did not dare to let her take a straight course. It was necessary to change her course in the combing seas, to meet them with what skill I could when they rolled up ahead, and to keep off when they came up abeam.

On the following morning, April 14, only the tops of the highest mountains were in sight, and the *Spray*, making good headway on a northwest course, soon sank these out of sight. 'Hurrah for the *Spray*!' I shouted to seals, seagulls, and penguins; for there were no other living creatures about, and she had weathered all the dangers of Cape Horn. Moreover, she had on her voyage round the Horn salved a cargo of which she had not jettisoned a pound. And why should not one rejoice also in the main chance coming so of itself?

I shook out a reef, and set the whole jib, for, having sea-room, I could square away two points. This brought the sea more on her quarter, and she was the wholesomer under a press of sail. Occasionally an old south-west sea, rolling up, combed athwart her, but did no harm. The wind freshened as the sun rose half-mast or more, and the air, a bit chilly in the morning, softened later in the day; but I gave little thought to such things as these.

One wave, in the evening, larger than others that had threatened all day, – one such as sailors call 'fine-weather seas', – broke over the sloop fore and aft. It washed over me at the helm, the last that swept over the *Spray* off Cape

Horn. It seemed to wash away old regrets. All my troubles were now astern; summer was ahead; all the world was again before me. The wind was even literally fair. My 'trick' at the wheel was now up, and it was 5 p.m. I had stood at the helm since eleven o'clock the morning before, or thirty hours.

Then was the time to uncover my head, for I sailed alone with God. The vast ocean was again around me, and the horizon was unbroken by land. A few days later the *Spray* was under sail, and I saw her for the first time with a jigger spread. This was indeed a small incident, but it was the incident following a triumph. The wind was still southwest, but it had moderated, and roaring seas had turned to gossiping waves that rippled and pattered against her sides as she rolled among them, delighted with their story. Rapid changes went on, those days, in things all about while she headed for the tropics. New species of birds came around; albatrosses fell back and became scarcer and scarcer; lighter gulls came in their stead, and pecked for crumbs in the sloop's wake.

On the tenth day from Cape Pillar a shark came along, the first of its kind on this part of the voyage to get into trouble. I harpooned him and took out his ugly jaws. I had not till then felt inclined to take the life of any animal, but when John Shark hove in sight my sympathy flew to the winds. It is a fact that in Magellan I let pass many ducks that would have made a good stew, for I had no mind in the lonesome strait to take the life of any living thing.

From Cape Pillar I steered for Juan Fernandez, and on the 26th of April, fifteen days out, made that historic island right ahead.

The blue hills of Juan Fernandez, high among the clouds, could be seen about thirty miles off. A thousand emotions thrilled me when I saw the island, and I bowed my head to the deck. We may mock the Oriental salaam, but for my part I could find no other way of expressing myself.

The wind being light through the day, the *Spray* did not reach the island till night. With what wind there was to fill her sails she stood close in to shore on the northeast side, where it fell calm and remained so all night. I saw the twinkling of a small light farther along in a cove, and fired a gun, but got no answer, and soon the light disappeared altogether. I heard the sea booming against the cliffs all night, and realized that the ocean swell was still great, although from the deck of my little ship it was apparently small. From the cry of animals in the hills, which sounded fainter and fainter through the night, I judged that a light current was drifting the sloop from the land, though she seemed all night dangerously near the shore, for, the land being very high, appearances were deceptive.

Soon after daylight I saw a boat putting out toward me. As it pulled near, it so happened that I picked up my gun, which was on the deck, meaning only to put it below; but the people in the boat, seeing the piece in my hands, quickly turned and pulled back for shore, which was about four miles distant. There were six rowers in her, and I observed that they pulled with oars in oar-locks, after the manner of trained seamen, and so I knew they belonged to a civilized race; but their opinion of me must have been anything but flattering when they mistook my purpose with the gun and pulled away with all their might. I made them understand by signs, but not without difficulty, that I did not intend to shoot, that I was simply putting the piece in the cabin, and that I wished them to return. When they understood my meaning they came back and were soon on board.

One of the party, whom the rest called 'king,' spoke English; the others spoke Spanish. They had all heard of the voyage of the *Spray* through the papers of Valparaiso, and were hungry for news concerning it. They told me of a war between Chile and the Argentine, which I had not heard of when I was there. I had just visited both countries, and I told them that according to the latest reports, while I was in Chile, their own island was sunk. (This same report that Juan Fernandez had sunk was current in Australia when I arrived there three months later.)

I had already prepared a pot of coffee and a plate of doughnuts, which, after some words of civility, the islanders stood up to and discussed with a will, after which they took the *Spray* in tow of their boat and made toward the island with her at the rate of a good three knots. The man they called king took the helm, and with whirling it up and down he so rattled the *Spray* that I thought she would never carry herself straight again. The others pulled away lustily with their oars. The king, I soon learned, was king only by courtesy. Having lived longer on the island than any other man in the world, — thirty years, — he was so dubbed. Juan Fernandez was then under the administration of a governor of Swedish nobility, so I was told. I was also told that his daughter could ride the wildest goat on the island. The governor, at the time of my visit, was away at Valparaiso with his family, to place his children at school. The king had been away once for a year or two, and in Rio de Janeiro had married a Brazilian woman who followed his fortunes to the far-off island. He was himself a Portuguese and a native of the Azores. He had sailed in New Bedford whale-ships and had steered a boat. All this I learned, and more too, before we reached the anchorage. The sea-breeze, coming in before long, filled the *Spray*'s sails, and the experienced Portuguese mariner piloted her to a safe berth in the bay, where she was moored to a buoy abreast the settlement.

V

The islanders at Juan Fernandez entertained with Yankee doughnuts – The beauties of Robinson Crusoe's realm – The mountain monument to Alexander Selkirk – Robinson Crusoe's cave – A stroll with the children of the island – Westward ho! with a friendly gale – A month's free sailing with the Southern Cross and the sun for guides – Sighting the Marquesas – Experience in reckoning.

The *Spray* being secured, the islanders returned to the coffee and doughnuts, and I was more than flattered when they did not slight my buns, as the professor had done in the Strait of Magellan. Between buns and doughnuts there was little difference except in name. Both had been fried in tallow, which was the strong point in both, for there was nothing on the island fatter than a goat, and a goat is but a lean beast, to make the best of it. So with a view to business I hooked my steelyards to the boom at once, ready to weigh out tallow, there being no customs officer to say, 'Why do you do so?' and before the sun went down the islanders had learned the art of making buns and doughnuts. I did not charge a high price for what I sold, but the ancient and curious coins I got in payment, some of them from the wreck of a galleon sunk in the bay no one knows when, I sold afterward to antiquarians for more than face-value. In this way I made a reasonable profit. I brought away money of all denominations from the island, and nearly all there was, so far as I could find out.

Juan Fernandez, as a place of call, is a lovely spot. The hills are well wooded, the valleys fertile, and pouring down through many ravines are streams of pure water. There are no serpents on the island, and no wild beasts other than pigs and goats, of which I saw a number, with possibly a dog or two. The people lived without the use of rum or beer of any sort. There was not a police officer or a lawyer among them. The domestic economy of the island was simplicity itself. The fashions of Paris did not affect the inhabitants; each dressed according to his taste. Although there was no doctor, the people were all healthy, and the children were all beautiful. There were about forty-five souls on the island all told. The adults were mostly from the mainland of South America. One lady there, from Chile, who made a flying-jib for the *Spray*, taking her pay in tallow, would be called a belle at Newport. Blessed island of Juan Fernandez! Why Alexander Selkirk ever left you was more than I could make out.

A large ship which had arrived some time before, on fire, had been stranded at the head of the bay, and as the sea smashed her to pieces on the rocks, after the fire was drowned, the islanders picked up the timbers and utilized them in the construction of houses, which naturally presented a ship-like appearance. The house of the king of Juan Fernandez, Manuel Carroza by name, besides resembling the ark, wore a polished brass knocker on its only door, which was painted green. In front of this gorgeous entrance was a flag-mast all ataunto, and near it a smart whale-boat painted red and blue, the delight of the king's old age.

I of course made a pilgrimage to the old lookout place at the top of the mountain, where Selkirk spent many days peering into the distance for the ship which came at last. From a tablet fixed into the face of the rock I copied these words, inscribed in Arabic capitals:

IN MEMORY
OF
ALEXANDER SELKIRK
MARINER,

A native of Largo, in the County of Fife, Scotland, who lived on this island in complete solitude for four years and four months. He was landed from the *Cinque Ports* galley, 96 tons, 18 guns, A.D. 1704, and was taken off in the *Duke*, privateer, 12th February, 1709. He died Lieutenant of H.M.S. *Weymouth*, A.D. 1723, aged 47. This tablet is erected near Selkirk's lookout, by Commodore Powell and the officers of H.M.S *Topaze*, A.D. 1868.

The cave in which Selkirk dwelt while on the island is at

the head of the bay now called Robinson Crusoe Bay. It is around a bold headland west of the present anchorage and landing. Ships have anchored there, but it affords a very indifferent berth. Both of these anchorages are exposed to north winds, which, however, do not reach home with much violence. The holding-ground being good in the first-named bay to the eastward, the anchorage there may be considered safe, although the undertow at times makes it wild riding.

I visited Robinson Crusoe Bay in a boat, and with some difficulty landed through the surf near the cave, which I entered. I found it dry and inhabitable. It is located in a beautiful nook sheltered by high mountains from all the severe storms that sweep over the island, which are not many; for it lies near the limits of the trade-wind regions, being in latitude 35½°S. The island is about fourteen miles in length, east and west; and eight miles in width; its height is over three thousand feet. Its distance from Chile, to which country it belongs, is about three hundred and forty miles.

Juan Fernandez was once a convict station. A number of caves in which the prisoners were kept, damp, unwholesome dens, are no longer in use, and no more prisoners are sent to the island.

The pleasant day I spent on the island, if not the pleasantest on my whole voyage, was my last day on shore, – but by no means because it was the last, – when the children of the little community, one and all, went out with me to gather wild fruits for the voyage. We found quinces, peaches, and figs, and the children gathered a basket of each. It takes very little to please children, and these little ones, never hearing a word in their lives except Spanish, made the hills ring with mirth at the sounds of words in English. They asked me the names of all manner of things on the island. We came to a wild fig-tree loaded with fruit, of which I gave them the English name. 'Figgies, figgies!' they cried, while they picked till their baskets were full. But when I told them that the *cabra* they pointed out was only a goat, they screamed with laughted, and rolled on the grass in wild delight to think that a man had come to their island who would call a cabra a goat.

The first child born on Juan Fernandez, I was told, had become a beautiful woman and was now a mother. Manuel Carroza and the good soul who followed him here from Brazil had laid away their only child, a girl, at the age of seven, in the little churchyard on the point. In the same half-acre were other mounds among the rough lava rocks, some marking the burial-place of native-born children, some the resting places of seamen from passing ships, landed here to end days of sickness and get into a sailors' heaven.

The greatest drawback I saw in the island was the want of a school. A class there would necessarily be small, but to some kind soul who loved teaching and quietude life on Juan Fernandez would, for a limited time, be one of delight.

On the morning of May 5, 1896, I sailed from Juan Fernandez, having feasted on many things but on nothing sweeter than the adventure itself of a visit to the home and to the very cave of Robinson Crusoe. From the island the *Spray* bore away to the north, passing the island of St Felix before she gained the trade-winds, which seemed slow in reaching their limits.

If the trades were tardy, however, when they did come they came with a bang, and made up for lost time; and the *Spray*, under reefs, sometimes one, sometimes two, flew before a gale for a great many days, with a bone in her mouth, toward the Marquesas, in the west, which she made on the forty-third day out, and still kept on sailing. My time was all taken up those days – not by standing at the helm; no man, I think, could stand or sit and steer a vessel round the world: I did better than that; for I sat and read my books, mended my clothes, or cooked my meals and ate them in peace. I had already found that it was not good to be alone, and so I made companionships with what there was around me, sometimes with the universe and sometimes with my own insignificant self; but my books were always my friends, let fail all else. Nothing could be easier or more restful than my voyage in the trade-winds.

I sailed with a free wind day after day, marking the position of my ship on the chart with considerable precision; but this was done by intuition, I think, more than by slavish calculations. For one whole month my vessel held her course true; I had not, the while, so much as a light in the binnacle. The Southern Cross I saw every night abeam. The sun every morning came up astern; every evening it went down ahead. I wished for no other compass to guide me, for these were true. If I doubted my reckoning after a long time at sea I verified it by reading the clock aloft made by the Great Architect, and it was right.

There was no denying that the comical side of the strange life appeared. I awoke, sometimes, to find the sun already shining into my cabin. I heard water rushing by, with only a thin plank between me and the depths, and I said, 'How is this?' But it was all right; it was my ship on her course, sailing as no other ship had ever sailed before in the world. The rush of water along her side told me that she was sailing at full speed. I knew that no human hand was at the helm; I knew that all was well with 'the hands' forward, and that there was no mutiny on board.

The phenomena of ocean meteorology were interesting studies even here in the trade-winds. I observed that about every seven days the wind freshened and drew several points farther than usual from the direction of the pole; that is, it went round from east-southeast to south-southeast, while at the same time a heavy swell rolled up from the southwest. All this indicated that gales were going on in the anti-trades. The wind then hauled day after day as it moderated, till it stood again at the normal point, east-southeast. This is more or less the constant state of the winter trades in latitude 12°S., where I 'ran down the latitude' for weeks. The sun, we all know, is the creator of the trade-winds and of the wind system over all the earth. But ocean meteorology is, I think, the most fascinating of all. From Juan Fernandez to the Marquesas I experienced six changes of these great palpitations of sea-winds and of the sea itself, the effect of far-off gales. To know the laws that govern the winds, and to know that you know them, will give you an easy mind on your voyage round the world, otherwise you may tremble at the appearance of every cloud. What is true of this in the trade-winds is much more so in the variables, where changes run more to extremes.

To cross the Pacific Ocean, even under the most favourable circumstances, brings you for many days close to nature, and you realize the vastness of the sea. Slowly but surely the mark of my little ship's course on the track-chart reached out on the ocean and across it, while at her utmost speed she marked with her keel still slowly the sea that carried her. On the forty-third day from land, – a long time to be at sea alone, – the sky being beautifully clear and the moon being 'in distance' with the sun, I threw up my sextant for sights. I found from the result of three observations, after long wrestling with lunar tables, that her longitude by observation agreed within five miles of that by dead-reckoning.

This was wonderful; both, however, might be in error, but somehow I felt confident that both were nearly true, and that in a few hours more I should see land; and so it happened, for then I made the island of Nukahiva, the southernmost of the Marquesas group, clear-cut and lofty. The verified longitude when abreast was somewhere between the two reckonings; this was extraordinary. All navigators will tell you that from one day to another a ship may lose or gain more than five miles in her sailing-account, and again, in the matter of lunars, even expert lunarians are considered as doing clever work when they average within eight miles of the truth.

I hope I am making it clear that I do not lay claim to cleverness or to slavish calculations in my reckonings. I think I have already stated that I kept my longitude, at least, mostly by intuition. A rotator log always towed astern, but so much has to be allowed for currents and for drift, which the log never shows, that it is only an approximation, after all, to be corrected by one's own judgment from data of a thousand voyages; and even then the master of the ship, if he be wise, cries out for the lead and the lookout.

Unique was my experience in nautical astronomy from the deck of the *Spray* – so much so that I feel justified in briefly telling it here. The first set of sights, just spoken of, put her many hundred miles west of my reckoning by account. I knew that this could not be correct. In about an hour's time I took another set of observations with the utmost care; the mean result of these was about the same as that of the first set. I asked myself why, with my boasted self-dependence, I had not done at least better than this. Then I went in search of a discrepancy in the tables, and I found it. In the tables I found that the column of figures from which I had got an important logarithm was in error. It was a matter I could prove beyond a doubt, and it made the difference as already stated. The tables being corrected, I sailed on with self-reliance unshaken, and with my tin clock fast asleep. The result of these observations naturally tickled my vanity, for I knew that it was something to stand on a great ship's deck and with two assistants take lunar observations approximately near the truth. As one of the poorest of American sailors, I was proud of the little achievement alone on the sloop, even by chance though it may have been.

I was *en rapport* now with my surroundings, and was carried on a vast stream where I felt the buoyancy of His hand who made all the worlds. I realized the mathematical truth of their motions, so well known that astronomers compile tables of their positions through the years and the days, and the minutes of a day, with such precision that one coming along over the sea even five years later may, by their aid, find the standard time of any given meridian on the earth.

To find local time is a simpler matter. The difference between local and standard time is longitude expressed in time – four minutes, we all know, representing one degree. This, briefly, is the principle on which longitude is found independent of chronometers. The work of the lunarian, though seldom practised in these days of chronometers, is beautifully edifying, and there is nothing in the realm of navigation that lifts one's heart up more in adoration.

Phoenix 60p Paperbacks

History/Biography/Travel
The Empire of Rome A.D. 98–190 *Edward Gibbon*
The Prince *Machiavelli*
The Alan Clark Diaries: Thatcher's Fall *Alan Clark*
Churchill: Embattled Hero *Andrew Roberts*
The French Revolution *E.J. Hobsbawm*
Voyage Around the Horn *Joshua Slocum*
The Great Fire of London *Samuel Pepys*
Utopia *Thomas More*
The Holocaust *Paul Johnson*
Tolstoy and History *Isaiah Berlin*

Science and Philosophy
A Guide to Happiness *Epicurus*
Natural Selection *Charles Darwin*
Science, Mind & Cosmos *John Brockman, ed.*
Zarathustra *Friedrich Nietzsche*
God's Utility Function *Richard Dawkins*
Human Origins *Richard Leakey*
Sophie's World: The Greek Philosophers *Jostein Gaarder*
The Rights of Woman *Mary Wollstonecraft*
The Communist Manifesto *Karl Marx & Friedrich Engels*
Birds of Heaven *Ben Okri*

Fiction
Riot at Misri Mandi *Vikram Seth*
The Time Machine *H. G. Wells*
Love in the Night *F. Scott Fitzgerald*

The Murders in the Rue Morgue *Edgar Allan Poe*
The Necklace *Guy de Maupassant*
You Touched Me *D. H. Lawrence*
The Mabinogion *Anon*
Mowgli's Brothers *Rudyard Kipling*
Shancarrig *Maeve Binchy*
A Voyage to Lilliput *Jonathan Swift*

POETRY

Songs of Innocence and Experience *William Blake*
The Eve of Saint Agnes *John Keats*
High Waving Heather *The Brontes*
Sailing to Byzantium *W. B. Yeats*
I Sing the Body Electric *Walt Whitman*
The Ancient Mariner *Samuel Taylor Coleridge*
Intimations of Immortality *William Wordsworth*
Palgrave's Golden Treasury of Love Poems *Francis Palgrave*
Goblin Market *Christina Rossetti*
Fern Hill *Dylan Thomas*

LITERATURE OF PASSION

Don Juan *Lord Byron*
From Bed to Bed *Catullus*
Satyricon *Petronius*
Love Poems *John Donne*
Portrait of a Marriage *Nigel Nicolson*
The Ballad of Reading Gaol *Oscar Wilde*
Love Sonnets *William Shakespeare*
Fanny Hill *John Cleland*
The Sexual Labyrinth (for women) *Alina Reyes*
Close Encounters (for men) *Alina Reyes*